Heavenly Bodies

Poems by Dona Luongo Stein

In Mario
Tanti auguri,
Dona

Jacaranda Press
1995

Acknowledgments

AIDS ANTHOLOGY: "Safe Sex"
College English: "Early Snow"
Denver Quarterly: "The Bison of Lascaux"
Five Fingers Review: "El Día de los Muertos"
The Journal: "Ivy"
Looking for Home: Women Writing About Exile: "Schüpfen" as "Searching for
   Schüpfen"
Mississippi Valley Review: "Mt. St. Helens"
mpc Journal: "The Chocolate Trees"
Peeling the Onion: "My Sister's Hair" as "Braiding My Sister's Hair"
Ploughshares: "Landscape With Bride"
Poems: A Celebration: "My Father Walks His Last Hunting Dog"
Poetry Digest: "Oscar Wilde in Leadville, Colorado"
POETS ON: "I Wonder Who's Kissing Her Now"; "Late"
Prairie Schooner: "Spring Semester"
Sackbut Press: "Postcard from China"
Santa Clara Review: "My Sister's Hair" as "Braiding My Sister's Hair"
Sojourner: "Moon" as "The moon wants its sea back"
Sycamore Review: "Winter"

My gratitude for a Massachusetts Arts Lottery Grant, to the Djerassi Foundation,
the MacDowell Colony, the Montalvo Center for the Arts, and the Corporation of
YADDO.

Special thanks to colleagues and friends for your interest, help, and encourage-
ment. You know who you are.

Library of Congress Catalog Card Number 95-94292
ISBN 1-884516-01-7

Jacaranda Press
3080 Olcott Street, Suite 115-D
Santa Clara, CA 95054-3217

Printed at The Geryon Press, Limited
Tunnel, NY 13848

Cover and title page photo: The Saturnian system.
This collage of the Saturnian system was prepared from images taken by Voyager
1 in November 1980. The collage shows Saturn rising behind Dione in the
forefront. Tethys and Mimas are fading in the distance to the right, Enceladus and
Rhea are off Saturns rings to the left, and Titanis is in its distant orbit at the top.

Photo Credit: NASA

Contents

Jupiter   1

Dangers of the Female   2

Postcard from China   3

Moon   4

Early Snow   5

"I Wonder Who's Kissing Her Now"   6

My Sister's Hair   7

The Chocolate Trees   8

Landscape With Bride   9

The Angel of Forgetting   10

Reparations   12

The Bison of Lascaux   13

The Perseids   14

Winter   16

Ivy   18

Schüpfen   19

Missing Dark Matter   20

My Father Walks His Last Hunting Dog   21

Late   22

Safe Sex   23

Heavenly Bodies   25

KAPU   26

Oscar Wilde in Leadville, Colorado   27

Wood Carver, Oaxaca   28

Mt. St. Helens   29

Spring Semester   30

El Día de los Muertos   32

After Sally Ride   34

for my mother
and in memory
for my father

Jupiter

(July, 1994)

Comet bombardment shows plumes of fire
then a dark ring at contact
the center sunken as in a miniature tire

Hard to imagine the center's a crater
miles and miles across, clouds of gas
if on Earth would devastate us later

Altering our climate as perhaps
happened eons ago, some say
shown by three-toed dinosaur tracks

Or by dinosaur eggs which photographed show
in one a dried fetus curled from head to tail
crowded by shell it would soon outgrow

Just as my grandchild curls, head bowed on its neck stem
spine arced, turning, tiny arm at its nose
in the ultrasound photo
both wait to fall into day, their eyes closed.

Dangers of the Female
(for Kathy)

Some species consume
the mate after coupling
or do without: starfish
squeeze invisible eggs
into the ocean and in a wilderness
of sea males release
their tiny sperm—
it happens without touch.

Those stories about females:
snakes for hair
that gazed at petrify.
Teeth like saws between our legs—
and beyond our dangerous gates
of bone, Circe alters
the species in love.

More often, mothers teach us
how to part, curl
our various-colored hair
or rescue us when they come to the door
as the car idles in the driveway
gather one baby and some clothes
while we turn a bruised face

take up the other child and leave
before he comes home from work.
Sometimes mothers remind us
we once gave to water
torn parts of Orpheus
that could no longer enslave,
could only remember and sing.

Postcard from China

The moon shines on the sleeping cows.
A white fence with a broken board
glows brighter, a gray horse dozing
whitens. Chickens, ducks stir
in the brazen moon. The dark side
of a house grows darker shadows
then sails out of the hill into light.
Even the hills have trouble staying
anchored to earth tonight as the spots
of dry seas ride into the waves
of heaven. Here you see the same
fine dust arch whitely into silence,
the moon drag its shadow along
as board, horse, house become their own.

Moon

The moon wants its sea back
wants all liquids to acknowledge
this mother; you can hear
the obedient corpuscles lean
toward heaven. Yes, the sea
once belonged with the moon;
you can feel it long
for that face of ash and stone,
rotating toward her empty beds.
You can see it drag
its children, heaving itself
from its earthly canyons
green and splendid for her approval,
face up like a little girl.
You can smell its fear the moon
will grow old, disappear.
Wild with foam, pumping light,
the sea is willing to be
a reflection. How methodically
it thrashes in the moon's
new light. You can even taste
the sediment of sacrifice
as it turns everything
her color, white.

Early Snow

(for my mother)

Smoking, wearing high heels and lipstick
      at thirteen
      because you're tall and have
as your step-mother says, "a big mouth"
the older kids take you to the dance
where you dance with all the high-school stars
      the actor, football player
      the comic, the scholar and
      the brother of your sixteen
      year old husband to be
      then because you get cornered
      by a wise-guy who's been
      drinking, presses into you
you look for your step-brother, wriggle away
      find him and his girl
      (you think it's she) in the parking lot
      but don't care to interrupt
so you sit on the running board
of someone's car for a smoke
while "Wonder where my baby is tonight"
      is squeezed out of a sax and
think about this new world, part of the same
world's October snow you'll run through
      pregnant, fifteen
      and late for school.

"I Wonder Who's Kissing Her Now"

My father would sing
on the way to Peterborough:
"I wonder who's lookin' into her eyes,
breathin' sighs, tellin' lies."
In the back seat
on that itchy fabric
I'd hold my breath
on nausea from the curves
from the confusion of his teasing

as he drew out "t-e-l-l-i-n' l-i-e-s"
in his fine tenor
as if he had a girl friend
she should be jealous of. She'd say "humph!"
and stare out her side window. He'd grin

and I'd see his gold tooth
glint in the rear-view mirror
as he'd call out, "How ya' doin' kiddo,
everything all right?"

"Wonder who's buyin' the wine,"
he'd continue, "for the lips that"
"Why don't you just shut up,"
she'd say, "and keep your mind
on the road, huh?" and he'd switch to:
"When Irish Eyes Are Smilin" while her green
perhaps Irish eyes turned on him.
If only she'd laughed,
or made believe she didn't care
and opened her red red lips to sing.

My Sister's Hair
(for Susie)

One strand loose, I go back, pick it up,
wind it over my finger and bind it in.
Not just love keeps me at this;
to have you still, tranced beneath my hands
as if obedient to my will—we must have been enchanted,
you by trust, me by duty, as I wound
measured widths in a fall of hair
so black its thick lengths shone blue.

One braid behind each ear, down the back
of your scalp the white path sharply parted
each side with a few short hairs curled
where the brown skin of your neck began.
We were both children, you three, me twelve—
it was my task to help mother so you could
go play—we sisters and brothers thought you
the favored child, beautiful, sweet,
how could we be mean? Yet jealousy and need
would not let us show our love. Your quietude
with my care let me learn what it is to love,
how anguish in tenderness gets caught,
trained, bound as in highlights
of hair so black it shines back blue.

The Chocolate Trees

In the candy store it rains chocolate.
All day, chocolate circulates through the air conditioner;
With chocolate in our nostrils, under our fingernails
        and on our tongues,
We stagger to closing time filled with the burden
        of sweetness: soft caramel, rough nougat
        and the slight alcohol of cherry cordial
For the boss encourages us two high schoolers, her clerks,
        to eat: "How will you know what's inside
        unless you taste it?" she asks.

Hip-deep in chocolate, I fill trays, wash
        my sticky hands often, avoid
        the candies I detest: coconut clusters,
        jellies, chocolate-covered ginger.

The boss's assistant leans near me at the back-room counter:
        "Who's your boyfriend? Do you have *lots* of boyfriends?"
She steps closer, "I bet you do have a boyfriend, huh?"
I take a side step away, watch my hands pack chocolates.
        When I say nothing, she says: "You'll find out
        what it's like, you'll see. And you'll want it
        all the time." Embarrassed, angry, I finish
Packing the box of candy then brush
        the chocolate tops to make them shine.
I avoid her eyes, keep out of her way
As I make out a shipping label and imagine
How I would stuff her with chocolates
I detest until she apologizes

Because every day after school and on Saturdays
Among chocolate truffles, dark chocolate turtles
        and bulbous chocolate-covered cherries
I felt excitingly rich, entranced
        as if under a parrot's blue wing
In a cocoa forest of the chocolate trees.

Landscape With Bride

Before an unintended war, she tends
to details: is the church ready,
where are the rings? The floating

homunculus curls into its body, still
abstract for her, and the man
dressed in rented white? Not ready
for war, for domestic trouble,
his dim fears that women unsex men.

Things that cost money worry him,
yet there's some saving with the old:
her grandmother's pearls, his
great-grandfather's ring, its worn gold
and stamped dates—how did it survive

such history? As war works closer
to their lives, the groom's restless,
nagged by green in the hills
of a late Northern spring. She greets him
under her mother's apple tree in bloom.

She is clear to him, he wants only
to make her happy—yes, her joy
will address his doubt, he will feel
comforted, pleased: this *is* what he wants.

He looks up through rings
of shadowed green, sees tree limbs
crossed like scissors
as his hand moves to hers, gloved, white.

The Angel of Forgetting

Today I went to look at water,
the sea between islands
not the green horizon
beyond where the buoy leans into waves

       Time shrinks my skeleton each day
and what comes after nightfall
fills the cave of my head with noise
like a wind off the sea enclosed.
I awake having forgotten—
that's a miracle, isn't it?

Remember the Bodhisattva
of Compassion, lotus bloom
at its midsection, the folds of garment
dropping like petals on the painted wood arms?
Full of repose, one knee bent
for the weight of an arm

one hand bent for the weight
of the upper body, the figure
from the Chinese Sung
of green and aged wood looked hauled
from the sea, made us think
Compassion is a balance in the universe

       Each time we approach, desire
makes us forget what we know
as if the act of love reinvents
flesh and breath and time.

Children learn to be women,
practice to be men, forget their anger
at being spirits in flesh
and start over again each day.

There must be an Angel of Forgetting
a short one with red hair
who holds up a garment to walk
in the sea, an island to the left,
one to the right, a buoy that leans
into waves clanging, clanging

      the same angel must have been there
when Bach forgot everything but form
wrote Variations for Clavier,
notes like stones washed by the sea
while the angel sat on the edge
of the instrument, tapped its foot
against painted wood.

      While restless and in pain
the Count who couldn't sleep
would call out from the next room:
"Dear Goldberg, do play one of my variations,"
and Goldberg would begin the aria,
its one change each bar,
as gradually the Count
would forget to remember.

Reparations
(The War Claims Act)

To Washington the money comes
but to prove he is who he says he is
he takes his papers and his blood

then stands at the Lincoln Memorial.
He looks down fields to other monuments
of freedom, thinks about his mother's
words: "you floated over rubble and water
to be born with rickets in America."
It was a cold Spring when the money first came—
blossoms rolled on cement—pfennigs, dimes.

He doesn't change his life, he sees it
as bought. His children don't spend
days in warehouses or at benches making chipboards,
nights in classrooms. Their health
astonishes him. Muscular, trim,
they have no religion, improve
their skiing, swim. He'd keep them
on his small suburban lawn
forever, if he could.

He doesn't tell them
of the noise, stench of boxcars
in dreams caused by his mother's words
nor what he'd seen years later:
flowers around the camp
that shook gold coins on the paths.
He doesn't tell them
where their money comes from,
how survivors stay quietly alive,
nor that she once said
first it was the *idea* of him
then in her arms his slightly crooked body
that kept her daily from screaming.

The Bison of Lascaux

While you sleep on the mauve
sofa with its wooden frame,
I draw your profile.
With your glasses off
and your mind sliding
about another world,
large flakes fall
outside against the gray bark
of an old oak and this room
fills with quiet, with pauses.

We are still young, I say,
as I rub out a wrong eyebrow,
as I try again what amazes—
the delicate structure
of your bones around the eye,
the narrow nose, the narrow
chin. There, I have it:
the look of mild surprise,

then the reddish hairline
and one ear folded, thin.
Working on your slumbering bulk
of rust sweater and burgundy slacks,
I recall the delicate feet
of the bison beneath those reddish-brown
strokes outlined in black.

I hear your breath, watch
as your leg jumps.
I remember your smell,
how the sides of the beast
moved even after it stopped
its struggle, how
the darkness closes in.

The Perseids

About mid-August the Perseid showers come.
We decide to stay up to see
orange, yellow, lilac, whitened
streaks that burn
through our sky then out.

Before we can, we decide
we can't carry on. I brood
about Audubon who wired
his beloved birds, fresh-killed,
to pose them before their colors faded.
No, I worry about Lucy
with their children, keeper of books,
correspondence, the farm, teaching—
and the birds, still warm,
strung on wires—as change
alters the ideal *and* the real.
Listen, my reality is this: gullible, wild-haired,
once again I agree to teach on the Island.
Everyone knows who visits, when.

You write I should take your things
to the dump. I watch as if
affection melts down and passion
strikes like this fire, leaving
its hole with ash at the edge.
Quick, I say to myself as paper feathers
curl in smoke, name the hundred flowers
beginning with the letter "M,"
my natural history of fascination.

I carry back from the dump
a dried milk-weed stalk, its triple
desiccated pods sculptural,
their backs gray, thorny,
the inside amber, silk-soft,
the membrane still attached mid-section
like dried skin, the other half gone.

The other half gone. Exploded, blown out
when seeds and hairs burst
taken by wind
whirled, spun, arced
filaments steadying seeds
like keels on boats or tails to kites

or the Perseids
from a constellation
for a man-god who slayed snake-haired
Medusa with a mirror
because her gaze turned men to stone

Now Perseids
burst above the Island
momentarily held like seeds
        their feathered trails
        in reality burnt-out stones
brilliant, exhaustible
love

Winter

(Villa Montalvo)

The grapefruit tree's globes shine through rain and mist.
Behind them rise the palms. Downstairs, the staff

Ties grapefruit-sized balls of silver
And gilds with silver ribbons

An enormous fir that fills the hall
With its scent. At night when I pass,

I imagine the tree's life juice stains
The wooden floor, dripping onto silver ribbons

But the next day the tree dignifies
The spotless floor while outside, jonquils

In green bud ready to bloom in January
Line the outer walkway. Everyone tells me

This is winter—mist, rain. Sometimes I stand
Near the great fir feeling something like kin,

As displaced. Where I'm from everything's iced over;
I'd felt my soul retreat while the heaviness

Of my violent century sank through my dreams.
I try to believe this is winter,

Wear sweaters indoors and out, twist oranges
Loose in their ripeness, give away my coat.

Now the staff removes the banked poinsettias
And pushes the stripped tree to a corner.

16

Slowly I discard restraint, forget dreams
Dragged from another latitude, learn to let

Tenderness flower. Grass just planted
On the south hillside sprouts like new hair

And friends say that what we see from foothills
To the Bay becomes green in rain's excess

Except for the patrolled cement
Of the Air Force's center for orbiting space craft.

"Don't you know? This area's Ground Zero,"
They laugh. "Not to worry, now."

The grapefruit tree's little fires burn through the rain.

Ivy

Disappointed, angry with the way
our country's leaders turn
from us, betray our common good and trust,
I put on gloves, take out the long-handled loppers
and head for the ivy. It's crept over
walls, the fence, and stretched across the driveway
since the last time I noticed—this morning?
Now, aiming for connecting stems, I bend
open the sharp, curved blades and from long handles
throw my weight into the cut,
and with shut blades pull the runners out.
I could do this for days—wirey stems choke
palm trees, the fuchsia, and inch up the carport post.
In the hurt of the day, I'm thinking I'd rather
have been born in a different time, a different place,
or back to the teen-aged argument with my parents,
not at all. As I straighten to pile cut ivy,
I recall Josefa, Goya's wife, her twenty babies
born mostly dead. How could she have kissed

knowing what would happen after? Yet Josefa,
who knew of his other women, raised the few children
who survived and chose to stay with Goya. Free
from tightening stems, the fuchsia looks naked
and the smallest palm may live. Josefa, I want to say
I've forgotten what brought me to these green mounds
but understand something of the choice
to stay, of struggle in any age of venality—
and yes, I see how the charge of energy
that wants to cut, clear out,
here becomes busyness and shaping
while earth moves by small degrees from day.

Schüpfen

It's not just Schüpfen she's looking for,
it's either something so large, like desire
for an absent love, or so small
like a hair, finding Schüpfen
will not do. Outside Berne's the place

to start, she thinks, but since the trip
may be too simple, the search end
too soon, she will start in Paris
on the train South and East
to the city near the village of her mother.

So little history to go on—
her mother an orphan raised
by neighbors, animals brought into the house,
skiing out second-story windows
for the few years of school. Each piece

of paper reveals a different name:
Marta Rose, Marie, Rosa and no last name,
just guesses from step-cousins. No fixed date
among the spread of years. Meadow, stream,
and beyond the railroad station, fields

stretch out to woods. It's the future
she wants to make whole for the grandchildren
to grow into. She will have made a circle,
will pull a fine thread from the past
through field, eidelweiss, goat bells

as she checks names on the mossed stones
in the churchyard then lists in brown ink
on baptismal books. She'll tell each child
if the flowers are spicy, odorless, or sweet
in Schüpfen, and if there's a name, the name.

Missing Dark Matter

"...dark matter or 'missing mass'
makes up 90% of the universe"
— Hugo Wahlquist, physicist

Why do we search the grand lost dust
of astral explosions as if we must
recover everything? Can't we leave

some things lost? Let them be unhooked,
hidden, wandering, let the three puzzles
of the universe stay unsolved—

must we know our world's creation?
Or why we have a large satellite
or why the sun rotates slower than it should?

The "Lone Cypress" leans out
in Monterey Bay, frail, comical
twisting from cleft rock

with no visible connection
to rooted earth. Perhaps our admiration
sustains it, like the lost roses

rosarians breed back, the Damasks
of ancient Rome, souvenirs of history.
Like them, we refuse loss, keep

the lion's paw shell, a hat, a shirt
as if we could feel again the weight
of arms or from the hatbrim smell

familiar hair—those astrophysicists
tell us dark matter exists,
holds galaxies together

so dark matter has to be out there
they know, they search for what is just missing.

My Father Walks His Last Hunting Dog

Your dead/drift in me—Johannes Bobrowski

They are at
the top of the hill;
the last sun halves my father's
head, cigar smoke

idly drifts into evening air.
Though still young, he is tired
of this life already;
his trousers hang loose
since his last imprisonment,
his eyes hold too much time.
The dog limps with arthritis
and it is always like this,
their two forms between
fall aspens trembling in quiet air.
My father's stride halts
the dog stops
yet I hear them breathing
side by side still.

Late
(for Ben)

Never on time, that's me. "Lost in a dream"
They used to say and nicknamed me "Speed"
For my slow traffic with dust, with knives
And spoons in soapy water. What did I know
About rebellion and sabotage
Or the slow subversion of politeness,
Of courting, of capitalism. My bosses
Gave me timecards, their hands traveled
Up my arms in filing rooms, their footfalls
Swung into aisles like pendulums
Back and forth, their weight pulling
Their black shoes across my orbit.
My lovers gave me watches,
First big ones, then pretty ones,
Then ones that beeped and talked.
They said they loved the way my hands
Took all night to travel the red routes
To their dreams, but by day they were busy
With schedules and when I looked,
Their faces had the numbers "3" and "9"
Near their ears. With one, my period
Was late and I got a child who grew
Into a man with a finch near one ear,
A heron near the other and hair
That lies down like feathers. He watches
A fingerling twitch in stream shadow,
Has a slow way with the wrench and the saw
And like me, he's never on time.

Safe Sex

At our ages, we can't recall
who all our partners were.
We keep remembering another.
You tell me about Jan
a housemate's girlfriend
on drugs; you went to bed once
you say, then more: an accident,
didn't mean to,
Tony wasn't home, she'd come in crying.
Her ex-husband had her kid
and wouldn't let her see him.
You only meant to comfort her, hold her.

You're washing spinach, suddenly get quiet.
"I was scared of getting involved.
She was too unstable, Tony was too straight,
he couldn't help. I think she really liked me.
I liked her too." I'm at the table
cutting mushrooms, think of lovers
I drifted from: the ones who drank too much,
wanted too much. "And you?" you ask
"there must be someone you forgot."
I sweep the stems into my hand
and turn to the can we keep for compost.
"Did I tell you about Mike?"
You shake your head. "I think he was in love
with an older man, but he never said,
just talked about him a lot, what a great painter
he was, they were going to see a painter
from Mexico who'd worked on the murals
with Rivera." We're both quiet.

I'm standing by the window back
in that time and place. "Why did you do it,"
you want to know. "He was sweet
and I was lonely"—at that I let it go.
"What happened," you ask. "I had to leave
for a job somewhere else."

      It starts
to get dark outside; between the table
and the sink two other people wait
for solace or denial once again. Surprised
I still hold mushroom stems
I move toward you. We hold each other
until there's just us
making the unlit kitchen
a small protected place.

Heavenly Bodies
(for Francisco)

"The best job I ever had was on
a turkey farm. I fed them, watered them,
and cleaned them. I had time to sit and dream.
I had time to read. Then a new boss came.
He no longer needed my expertise. I think
he was prejudiced because I am a dark Hispanic.
He was Hispanic too but this happens you know.
The turkeys didn't care what I am,
I kept them clean and full and warm.

The worst job I ever had is the job I have now.
I am a ticketer in a factory.
Everything we do is counted
and we are watched. I do not dare to go
to the bathroom. I get so nervous
I do not like to sit to eat and besides
we don't have much time to eat. At this job
the boss goes back and forth
over my soul. My body is sad and weeps.

The job I will be looking for
is an astronomer, a specialist
in comets and giant stars. I have
my own telescope. I sit on the sidewalk
in front of my house and look for hours.
I can be a specialist in comets
and giant stars, I know where they are."

KAPU
(Punaluu, Hawai'i)

KAPU! slant-painted in red
faces the black sand beach
where hawksbills swim
where, Anu says in disgust,
she's seen them dead, naked,
hacked from their shells
because Japan and Mexico
still buy them. KAPU! Taboo,
no trespassing, stay off, sacred.
This owner speaks for him or herself
for the land, the table, crooked chair,
piled boxes, rusted VW bus, small
wooden boat atilt on a trailer.
KAPU Anu says also means
something or someone will
repay you for what you do.

26

Oscar Wilde in Leadville, Colorado

He approached the stage languidly
like a love-sick girl
and dressed in a green gown, held
a flower, swayed to the reading stand.
We knew he was different but the difference
stunned us, made those who would laugh
cough instead. He welcomed us

in the stuffy hall smelling of sweat
and soap, spoke to us without paper.
He had everything memorized out.
He didn't speak long, he finished
with Silene's words

which impressed many of us so we went
up after to ask him to introduce us.
Gently, he explained Silene had died
then accepted our invitation to dine
at the bottom of the mine. We lowered

him in a slag bucket to the mayor
and other worthies waiting then passed
around bottles of whiskey which he drank
from at every round. He pulled on the rope
to be hauled up but no one else came

after him, they'd all passed out.
The only thing to do was elect him
Honorary Citizen of Leadville for Life
and hail him worthy of our affection
so we sang "For He's a Jolly Good Fellow"
while the mayor and others slept
in the mine for the night.

Wood Carver, Oaxaca

He uses the machete
to hack at the chunk
of wood, turning it

turning it in one hand
while he hacks with
the other then rests

then rests it on his knees
still turning and hacking.
As we watch wood becomes

a hump-backed long-snouted
armadillo, a creature
from the isthmus,

the damp south next to Chiapas
where people lie lined up on the ground
their hands tied behind their backs

with wire. Armadillo
legs emerge from shell, shell
and legs that these hands will paint

with dots, stripes, and stars.

Mt. St. Helens
(erupted May 1980)

Tagged salmon avoided the ash-filled Cowlitz
showed up at the next clear river,
the Kalama. Only weeks later
fresh animal tracks were seen—
where did they come from?
Shoots of pearly everlasting,
horsetail rushes, beargrass, fireweed,
pushed through crusty layers of ash.
Underground animals—pocket gophers,
mice, and ants—survived the blanket
of sulphurous ash aglow,
no one knows how. Perhaps tunnels
trapped oxygen (divers know spaces
in our bodies hold air as if our cells
in urgency absorb and breathe).
How different from what we told
ourselves when we saw the blackened sky
in full day: "Now they've done it,"
we said and moved about numb,
already mourning, not yet for our children
or ourselves but for things
we didn't know we loved—the worn path
beneath the lines of drying sheets
now gray with fallen ash.

Spring Semester

You have to acknowledge, my office mate says,
the sadness of departure, of leaving;

a little *tristesse* without the pleasure
of touch, I want to add. This semester's

been hard with students on their way out
of childhood confiding their difficult lives

cheerfully as they left behind stoop labor
with nine brothers and sisters

in the berry fields I've seen stretch
to the sea so the bright triangular gems

in the market can't be lifted without
thinking of the bent backs that put them there

still moving between endless rows, eyes
stinging with sweat. Their narrations

this semester consign uncles who touched
them where they shouldn't have

to forgiveness—they wrote they know
at twenty-six what despair pushes love to

now that they have four kids of their own.
Their specific details described alleys

they woke up in before being saved
and now sober and clean, they argued

for self-help and the praise of higher powers.
At the final conference, despite

homes still on jacks from earthquake damage,
they are eager for next semester

having "learned a lot" and "liked the course"—
so did their wives and boy-friends who read

their papers and corrected spelling errors.
I'm tired, have only lately consigned

the strangers who touched me to limbo and still don't know
what to make of the years alcohol ate,

when the last student brings flowers—
the freesia, anemone, and baby mums

releasing in the space between us
scents both acrid and slightly sweet.

El Día de los Muertos
(November 2)

For my father, the unlucky one,
forgiver of life, the candle
in my right hand
for my grandmother of secrets
who died with the name
of her Japanese lover
locked behind her teeth,
the candle in my left hand

and for myself, my face painted white
eye sockets blackened, mouth
rimmed black, I march
beneath piñatas
among bins of calaveras, conchas, churros

we prepare to wake
from this life
where even the torturers
the police my father forgave
will be identified
by their knuckles and silence

he taught me
it is not justice I must seek
but truth
so I celebrate
the way he gambled and sang and wrote us
from jail
and my Swiss grandmother's closed lips
after her lover
left her pregnant in Mexico

we pass the stand of nopales
reminded by candlelight and sweat
how short the cycle
up the hill
ghastly apparitions
I swear by
my father's limp, his missing fingers,
his clouded left eye
to seek truth

I swear by his clear voice
urging me to forget Justice
whose bound and jealous eyes
must guess the shape of truth
in its sour, its sweet noise

to keep moving
I shift my arm
protect the flame, the candle
in my right hand for my father
in my left hand
for my grandmother

After Sally Ride

What is it like
to look back at Earth
from twelve miles up?
There's a halo
that we can see
around our planet
that rarely shows
in photographs
and we don't know
what causes it,
but we also know
that living cells
under the microscope
have a halo
around them
and we don't know
why that is either
or why painters
put haloes
around the heads
of saints
and angels
or why people
who have near-death
experiences
report
that loved ones
who have died
and greet them
appear
with haloes
as if their having been
important
in their lives

sanctifies
their flesh
as the living cell
and our planet
are more than
sources
of light
as if all
the living
in one cell,
on one planet,
causes
a halo,
the halo
I saw from the port
of the spaceship
looking back
at Earth.

Dona Luongo Stein was born in Boston, Massachusetts and educated at Tufts University, Clark University, Harvard University, and Warren Wilson College. A former Stegner Fellow at Stanford University, her first collection, *Children of the Mafiosi,* was published by West End Press. She lives in Aptos, California and teaches at Cabrillo College.